Write Now!

Elaine Canham

OXFORD
UNIVERSITY PRESS

OXFORD
UNIVERSITY PRESS

Great Clarendon Street, Oxford OX2 6DP

Oxford University Press is a department of the University of Oxford.
It furthers the University's objective of excellence in research, scholarship,
and education by publishing worldwide in

Oxford   New York

Auckland   Cape Town   Dar es Salaam   Hong Kong   Karachi
Kuala Lumpur   Madrid   Melbourne   Mexico City   Nairobi
New Delhi   Shanghai   Taipei   Toronto

With offices in

Argentina   Austria   Brazil   Chile   Czech Republic   France   Greece
Guatemala   Hungary   Italy   Japan   Poland   Portugal   Singapore
South Korea   Switzerland   Thailand   Turkey   Ukraine   Vietnam

Oxford is a registered trade mark of Oxford University Press
in the UK and in certain other countries

Text © Elaine Canham 2005

The moral rights of the author have been asserted

Database right Oxford University Press (maker)

First published 2005

British Library Cataloguing in Publication Data

Data available

ISBN 978-0-19-919881-8

21 23 25 27 29 30 28 26 24 22

Printed in China by Imago

Acknowledgements

The publisher would like to thank the following for permission to reproduce
photographs: **p4**l Corbis/David Lees, r Corbis/Bettmann, **p5** Classet/OUP, **p6** Ancient Art &
Architecture, **p9** The Petrie Museum of Egyptian Archaeology at University College, London,
p10t Corbis/Patrick Ward, **p11** Heritage Museum/British Museum, **p12** Mary Evens Picture
Library/Bruce Castle Museum, **p14** Corbis, **p15** Science Photo Library/Library of Congress, **p16**
Corbis, Adam Woolfitt, **p17**t Corbis/Maull & Polyblank, b Corbis/Bettman, **p18** Mary Evans
Picture Library, **p20** Corbis/Hulton Deutsch Collection, **p21**t Imperial War Museum, b Corbis/Pat
Jerrold; Papilio, **p22** Corbis/Hulton Deutsch Collection, **p23**t Imperial War Museum,
b Corbis/Bettmann, **p24**r Alamy, **p25** Corbis/Ted Soqui, **p27** Classet/OUP, **p28** Corbis/Paul
Seheult; Eye Ubiquitious, **p30** Corbis

Cover: OUP

Illustrations by Chris Brown: **p6**, **p8**; Mark Draisey: **p7**, **p26**, **p29**; Stefan Chabluk: **p10**, **p17**

Extracts from *Dearest Child: Letters between Queen Victoria and the Princess Royal,
Previously Unpublished* edited by Roger Fulford (Henry Holt and Co, Inc.),
copyright © Roger Fulford 1964, 1992, reprinted by permission of the publishers.

Extract from *Wilfred Owen: Collected Letters* edited by Harold Owen and John Bell (OUP, 1967),
reprinted by permission of Oxford University Press.

Every effort has been made to contact copyright holders of material reproduced in this book. If notified,
the publishers will be pleased to rectify any errors or omissions at the earliest opportunity.

Contents

We all write letters   4
We all need to keep in touch

Any complaints   6
Even the King of Babylon
could have a bad day

Dead letters   8
Some of the earliest known
letters are from Egyptians
to their dead relatives

Ordinary life   10
A birthday invitation from
a Roman soldier's wife

The Royal Mail   12
King Charles II invented it
to cut costs – and then he
got bills through the post

Write on   14
Alexander Graham Bell
invented the telephone,
but he had to write a letter
to tell his father

Royal stamp of approval   16
Queen Victoria loved
writing letters

Postcards   18
They were the Victorians'
text messages

Letters from the front   20
A lifeline to home from
soldiers in the First
World War

The first air mail   22
Pigeon post takes off

Taking to the air   24
The text–messaging
revolution

Writing on the Web   26
Email to you and me

A mixed bag   28
The odd things you
find in the post

How to jazz up your letters   30
How to decorate your
letter paper – and add
an air of mystery!

Glossary   31

Index   32

We all write letters

Imagine you lived thousands of years ago and you wanted to keep in touch with your friends when they were far away. What would you do? Use smoke signals? Beat jungle drums? Hmm, bit awkward if you wanted to have a good gossip.

What people did, of course, was to learn how to make marks that could be understood by everyone; they invented writing. Writing meant they could share thoughts and ideas, even when they were apart.

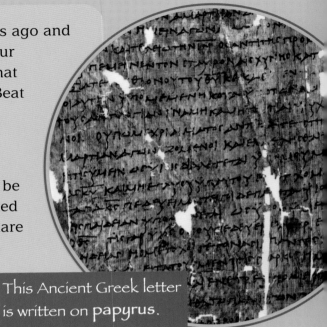

This Ancient Greek letter is written on **papyrus**.

The earliest letters were scratched on clay tablets and then had to be left to dry, like bricks. Now we have emails which take seconds to write and send. But the things people write about never really change. People write to tell stories, to explain what has been happening to them, to thank someone, or even to complain. They write to send their love, to wish someone a happy day or maybe congratulate them.

This Babylonian clay tablet looks like a bird has walked all over it – but it shows one of the earliest form of writing called cuneiform.

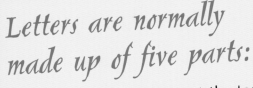

Letters are normally made up of five parts:

1. the address and date at the top

2. the greeting: Dear So and so

3. the body: this is the message you want to write

4. the close: Yours sincerely, Yours faithfully, or maybe just Love from

5. the signature line: if it's a business letter, you type your name and sign above it. If it's a letter to a friend, you just sign your name.

Forgotten something?

Put the initials PS at the end, and then write what you want to add. PS stands for 'post script', which is Latin for 'after writing'.

Any complaints?

Lots of people today write letters to complain when things go wrong. They write to the railway company if their trains are late, or to a manufacturing firm if something they have bought – like a washing machine – doesn't work. Lots of organisations have departments specially set up to deal with complaints. They're called 'Customer Services'.

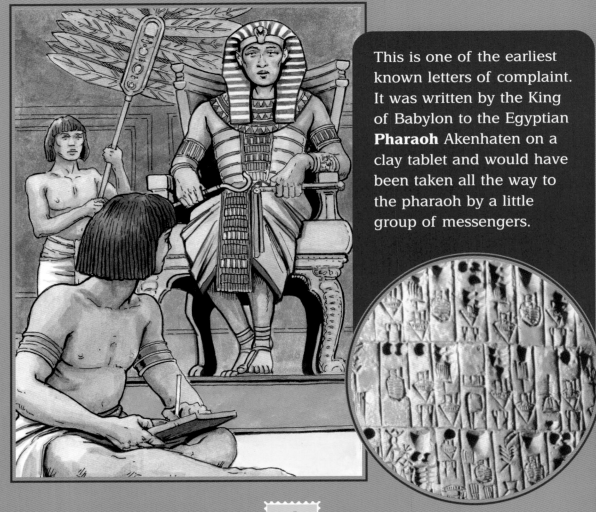

This is one of the earliest known letters of complaint. It was written by the King of Babylon to the Egyptian **Pharaoh** Akenhaten on a clay tablet and would have been taken all the way to the pharaoh by a little group of messengers.

'And the men who murdered my slaves, kill them and avenge their blood. Because if you do not kill these men, they will again murder ... If this should happen the people of the land will leave you.'

The King of Babylon is complaining that his slaves were robbed and killed in Canaan, and he wants **revenge**. It is not known what the pharaoh replied.

How to complain

If something is bothering you, and you want to write a letter of complaint, remember to:

- find out the full name and address of the company or organization you need to contact

- say clearly in your first sentence what you are complaining about

- say what you want done. If possible, say what you will do if you don't get what you want. (You might go to a lawyer, or you might get a newspaper or radio station to tell everyone how you have been treated)

- be polite.

Dead letters

The Egyptians wrote letters to dead relatives. They believed the dead were very powerful and could help them solve really urgent problems. Some of the messages were written on linen or papyrus, but they have been mostly found on bowls. Egyptians felt that if things were going wrong, it was generally because they had offended someone who had just died, and their letters often reminded the dead that they treated them well when they were alive. The problems they wanted help with ranged from ill health to disputes over property. The dead person was expected to somehow help them sort out the problem.

This bowl is from a man called Shepsi to his dead parents for help in a row with his brother over **property**. He writes on the inside of the bowl to his father, with a message on the outside to his mother. To his father, Iinekhenmut, he says:

'Am I to be injured in your presence, without this your son having done or said anything, by my brother? … He has done this against this your son evilly, evilly.'

To his mother he writes:

'This is a reminder of the time that you said to this your son "Bring me quails for me to eat", and when this your son brought to you seven quails for you to eat. If only you would judge between me and Sobekhotep! I brought him from another town, and placed him in his town among his male and female dead, and gave him burial cloth. Why then is he acting against this your son, when I have said and done nothing, evilly, evilly?'

If you feel strongly about something, why not write a letter? You probably won't be able to get the dead to help you, but there's nothing to stop you from writing to the Queen, the Prime Minister, or your local MP (look up the address in a telephone directory under 'Members of Parliament'). What's more, you are almost certain to get a reply.

Ordinary life

When the Romans came to Britain common soldiers wrote to distant relatives and friends describing their lives, ordering food, complaining about mistreatment, and even sending birthday invitations.

Many of these letters, written in the first and second centuries, have been found at the fort of Vindolanda, just south of Hadrian's Wall, near the border of Scotland and England. They were written in ink on postcard-sized sheets of wood. One from Claudia Severa, the wife of the **garrison** commander Aelius Brocchus, asks a sister to come for her birthday. It is one of the earliest letters written by a Roman woman that has been found.

'Claudia Severa to her Lepidina greetings. On 11 September, sister, for the day of the celebration of my birthday, I give you a warm invitation to make sure that you come to us, to make the day more enjoyable for me by your arrival, if you are present. Give my greetings to your Cerialis. My Aelius and my little son send him their greetings. I shall expect you, sister. Farewell, sister, my dearest soul, as I hope to prosper, and hail.'

Nowadays you don't have to write on a piece of wood to send a birthday invitation. You can buy one already printed, and all you have to do is fill in the details. But if you want to write your own, like Claudia Severa, remember to:

- say how you are planning to celebrate your birthday, for example, if you are going swimming, or wearing fancy dress

- put the place, date and time of the party

- send it in plenty of time before the party

- make sure your friends tell you whether they are coming by putting the letters RSVP at the bottom of the invitation. They stand for 'Répondez s'il vous plaît', which is French for 'please reply'.

You are invited to come to my birthday party
at 4 Churchill Drive
on 14 July
starting at 2.00pm
Bring your swimming costume and a towel!
R.S.V.P. 7 July

The Royal Mail

Until King Charles II came to the throne, ordinary people found it difficult to send letters. Unless you were rich and powerful and had your own messengers, it was practically impossible to get news to anyone far away. In any case, few people could read and write. Then Charles II invented the Royal Mail – partly because he wanted other people to help pay for all the messengers he used.

One letter that he received was from his **portrait** painter, David des Granges, who hadn't been paid. In 1671, close to death, he begged Charles II for what he was owed.

In his letter he says how he has served the king 'faithfully and diligently' with his 'eyesight and labour failing him'.

The king agreed to pay up, but Mr Des Granges died soon after, and no one knows if he ever got the money.

Restauration: Charles II was the son of Charles I who was beheaded by Oliver Cromwell. Charles II became king in 1660 after Cromwell died. This was called the Restoration.

David des Granges' portrait of Charles II.

accompt: this comes from the French, meaning account, or bill.

threescore and sixteen: a score is twenty, so Des Granges was asking for £76 for several paintings. Nowadays each one of his miniatures is worth about £20,000.

'I have served your majesty faithfully and diligently before your restauration as your limner (painter) in Scotland, on accompt of which service there became due to your petitioner the summ of threescore & sixteen pounds for several pieces of work by him done and delivered to sundry persons of quality by Your Majesties own hands or your express order.'

Write on

On March 10, 1876 a man called Alexander Graham Bell wrote a letter to his father describing his latest invention – the telephone. Now millions of people have telephones and can keep in touch easily with relatives and friends. But Bell's invention did not mean the end of letters.

Nearly 130 years later we are still writing to each other. Sometimes when we want to explain something it is easier and clearer to write it down – and we can include diagrams. Of course Bell couldn't ring his father to explain what he had done – he had the only telephone in the world!

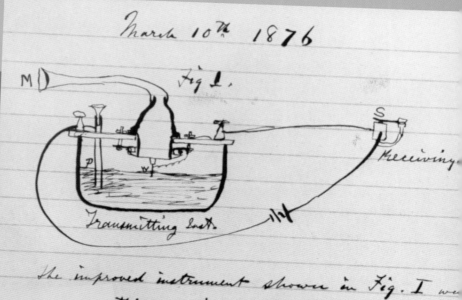

March 10th 1876

Fig 1.

M

S

Receiving

P W

Transmitting Inst.

The improved instrument shown in Fig. I w~~
this morning and tried this evening
~s pipe and W ~~the~~ platinum wir~
~th piece — and S the armature

Dear Papee

…I have constructed a new **apparatus** operated by the human voice. It is not of course complete yet — but some sentences were understood this afternoon. I was in one room at the **Transmitting** Instrument and Mr Watson at the Receiving Instrument in another room — out of earshot. I called out into the Transmitting Instrument; "Mr Watson — come here — I want to see you" — and he came!'

If you want to write an explanation, remember to:

● try to be as clear as possible

● say what you were aiming to do and what actually happened

● include your thoughts and feelings to make your explanation more vivid.

Don't forget you could add a diagram if it makes your explanation easier to understand.

Royal stamp of approval

In Victorian times, more and more people began to travel away from home. Britain was at the heart of the world's greatest **empire**, railways were being built and there was a huge demand for a simple efficient postal service.

Rowland Hill came up with the idea that you should pay for your letters when you sent them, by buying a stamp. Until then you were expected to pay for your letters when you got them – and many people refused. Queen Victoria, whose picture appeared on the Penny Black – the very first stamp – was a keen letter writer.

Rowland Hill

POST OFFICE REGULATIONS

ON AND AFTER THE 10th January a LETTER NOT EXCEEDING HALF AN OUNCE IN WEIGHT MAY BE SENT FROM ANY PART OF THE UNITED KINGDOM TO ANY OTHER PART FOR **ONE PENNY** IF PAID WHEN POSTED OR FOR **TWO PENCE** IF PAID WHEN DELIVERED

She wrote about her son Leopold, born in 1853 who was six at the time:

'Leopold… is the ugliest… He walks shockingly… and is dreadfully awkward… holds himself as badly as ever and his manners are despairing, as well as his speech… which is quite dreadful. It is so provoking as he learns so well and reads quite fluently; but his French is more like Chinese than anything else; poor child, he is really very unfortunate.'

Queen Victoria, seated, with Prince Albert and some of their children and servants.

Postcards

Postcards were the closest thing the Victorians could get to today's text messages or emails. People could send a quick message cheaply. There were several postal deliveries a day in most areas, so a postcard sent in the morning could arrive by that afternoon.

The first plain ones went on sale in the UK in October 1870. Firms soon worked out how to reproduce photographs on postcards and a boom began. Several hundred million postcards a year were bought not just for posting but also for collecting. Pictures of theatre and music hall stars were particularly popular.

This card shows Zena Dare, an actress. She autographed it, and on the back asks the person to whom she has given it to make a donation to a charity.

K6H5   AOBM

86GG2G   OBI

P2GH   9CJ2

However, anyone could read a postcard, and some people wrote their messages in simple code to make them more private.

This one means 'with many kisses and best wishes'.

Letters from the front

Some of the most haunting letters are those written by soldiers to their families. We know that even Roman soldiers wrote home. But until the First World War, soldiers tended to be sent to countries far away and their letters would be few and far between.

However, in 1914, when the war began, most people could read and write. France was close and the army postal service was quite efficient. It meant that soldiers could easily keep in touch, but people at home for the first time began to realise the true horror of war.

This letter was written by Wilfred Owen, who became famous for his poems about the cruelty, and waste, of war.

He wrote home to his mother:

...I can see no excuse for deceiving you about these last four days. I have suffered seventh hell.

I have not been at the front. I have been in front of it.

I held an advanced post, that is, a "dug-out" in the middle of No Man's Land. We had a march of three miles over shelled road, then nearly three along a flooded trench. After that we came to where the trenches had been blown flat out and had to go over the top. It was of course dark, too dark, and the ground was not mud, not sloppy mud, but an octopus of sucking clay, 3, 4, and 5 feet deep, relieved only by craters full of water...

Wilfred was sent to France in 1917, but became badly **concussed** after a shell landed just two yards away from him. He had to spend several days in a bomb crater with the mangled body of a fellow officer, and was sent to hospital in Scotland suffering from shell shock.

He was thought fit for duty again in August 1918 and was sent back to France. He was awarded the Military Cross for bravery, but died in a machine gun attack, seven days before the end of the war, aged 25.

It was very dangerous to show a light if you were in the trenches, so many soldiers used glow worms to read their letters from home.

NOTHING is to be written on this side except the date and signature of the sender. Sentences not required may be erased. If anything else is added the post card will be destroyed.

[Postage must be prepaid on any letter or post card addressed to the sender of this card.]

I am quite well.

I have been admitted into hospital
{ *sick* } *and am going on well.*
{ *wounded* } *and hope to be discharged soon.*

I am being sent down to the base.

I have received your { *letter dated* _____
                         telegram ,, _____
                         parcel ,, _____

Letter follows at first opportunity.

I have received no letter from you
{ *lately*
{ *for a long time.*

Signature }
only }

Date _____
Wt.W65—P.P.948. 8000m. 5-18. C. & Co., Grange Mills, S.W.

The army also censored soldiers' mail. This meant that officers would read all the letters going back to Britain to make sure there was no information that could help any spies. They would cut out things from the letters they didn't like. This process took a long time, and to speed things up soldiers were given special postcards that were supposed to get to their families more quickly.

The first air mail

Carrier pigeons have the amazing ability to find their way home from hundreds of miles away.

Egyptians and Persians used carrier pigeons 3000 years ago as the fastest way of sending messages. They can fly up to about 100 kilometres per hour for up to about 1000 kilometres (600 miles). The sender would place the message inside a tube attached to the pigeon's leg and then release it.

An army captain in 1941 with a carrier pigeon.

Pigeons have also been used as messengers in battles for thousands of years. They were used as recently as the first Gulf War in 1991. Until email became commonplace, the Indian government used more than 700 birds to help police in 400 stations communicate with each other.

Pigeons played an important role in communications during the two World Wars.

An American carrier pigeon called Cher Ami was shot through the breast but managed to deliver his message before dying. This led to the rescue of 194 men. He was awarded a French medal. A war memorial in Lille, France, commemorates 20,000 military pigeons killed during the First World War.

During the Second World War every RAF flight left England with two pigeons on board, which the crew could release if they got into difficulties, giving the location if the plane came down. A pigeon called Winkie flew 129 miles with her wings clogged with oil to save a downed bomber crew.

The Resistance Movement in France used carrier pigeons and one called Paddy brought back the first news of the D-Day invasion.

He, Winkie, and another pigeon, Mary of Exeter, were awarded the Dickin Medal – the animals' Victoria Cross for bravery.

Dickin Medal

Mary joined the pigeon service in 1940 and although she was wounded three times and received a total of 22 stitches, she flew missions until the end of the war. Mary had part of her wing shot off, underwent a major operation to remove three pellets from her body, and was badly injured by an attack from a hawk, specially kept for this purpose by German soldiers. But on each occasion she managed to find her way home.

Taking to the air

When you write a text, or an email, what happens to them and where do they go?

Texting

Your mobile phone is not really a phone at all; it is a small, very complicated radio transmitter and receiver – and a computer all rolled into one.

1 First tap out your text and press 'Send'. Your phone turns your text into digital code and sends it to the nearest cell, or base, station.

2 This is a base station. Do you see those panels on the mast? They receive your message and then transmit it from the dish. There are thousands of these stations all over the country. They form a sort of web so that it is very easy to pass on messages.

3 Your message, still in code, goes to a telephone hub. This is usually a building with a Short Message Service (SMS) computer. The computer checks if the person's phone you are calling is switched on.

4 If it is, your message travels through the web of antennae covering the country until it reaches the one nearest the person you are calling.

5 The phone that you are calling turns the digital code back into text and your message comes up on the screen.

Martin Cooper, 74, invented the mobile phone more than 30 years ago while working for Motorola. His telephone weighed one kilogram and his first call was made on April 3, 1973 while he was standing on a New York pavement.

The technology was then in place for people to have phones in their cars, but he wanted to make a personal telephone that anybody could carry anywhere. The first phone was put on sale in 1983 and cost £1500 (the equivalent of about £3000 today).

But Mr Cooper wouldn't use a mobile phone himself until they became small and light enough for him to wear on his belt. His phone now weighs less than 100 grams.

Writing on the Web

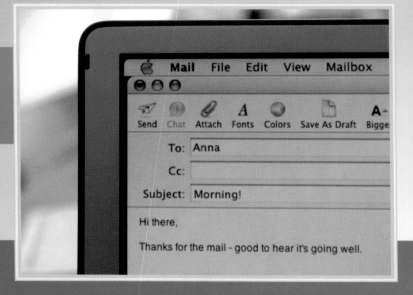

Sending an email is a complicated business for a computer.

Email

1. When you have typed your message and pressed the 'Send' button, the computer changes the message into a digital code and your email is sent to your Internet Service Provider (like BT or AOL).

2. Computers here check the email address (just like mail workers in a postal sorting office) and this tells them where to send the message.

3. Another computer cuts it up into little pieces all the same size. It puts a label on each piece saying where it belongs in the message, where it has come from and where it is going.

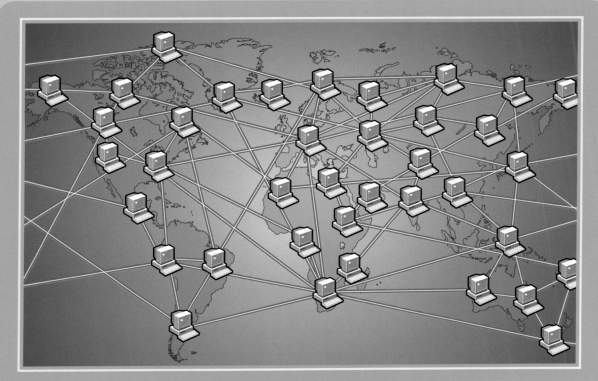

4   Your email is then put on the Internet. The Internet is made of millions of computers all over the world connected together. Each bit of the message can be sent a different way, using space satellites, telephone cables laid under the sea, microwave and fibre optics.

5   But when it arrives all the bits of the message are stuck back together again. The computer of the person you are emailing decodes the digital message and up pops your email on their screen. Bits of your message may have been all over the world but it will have taken only a few seconds to arrive.

A mixed bag

Today email has speeded things up, but people in Britain still send and receive 21 billion letters every year. And every year 72 million letters and parcels can't be delivered because they have no clear address. The Royal Mail has a special office in Belfast called the National Return Letter Centre where 300 workers try to work out where the letters were meant to go.

Often they have found quite strange things inside the parcels – including a live snake, a wooden leg and a **mummified** hand!

Many people have taken courses, and studied by post. These are called correspondence courses. The first organisation to offer them was Pennsylvania State University in 1886. The Open University began in the UK in Britain in the 1960s; people could learn from watching lectures on the TV and then writing **essays** and sending them in. Nowadays most students send their work via email.

Remember

- When you send a letter, write the name of the person you are writing to, and their address, clearly on the front of the envelope.

- Put your address on the back, so it can be returned to you if it can't be delivered.

- Include the postcode.

How to jazz up your letters

So why not start writing your own letters? They don't have to look boring. There's plenty of beautiful paper available, or you could always use plain white paper and decorate it.

You can use rubber stamps to create a repeating pattern down one or both margins and you could design your own letterhead. And don't forget to use a nice pen. You can even get **stationery** for your emails.

And if you want to add an air of mystery, why not write in code or invisible ink? You can make up simple codes by substituting letters for numbers, but make sure the person you are writing to knows how to decode it! A simple invisible ink is lemon juice. Just write your message with the juice and when you want to read it hold it next to a radiator – the heat will make the words appear.

Envelopes were invented by the Victorians – before then people simply stuck their letter together with sealing wax – often using a metal seal with a special design on it. You can still buy sealing wax and seals.

Why not try making your own envelopes? This Internet website has some unusual ideas: http://www.ghh.com/elf/.

Glossary

apparatus – piece of equipment

concussed – to become unconscious

empire – a group of countries ruled by a single person

essay – a piece of writing on a particular subject

garrison – troops stationed in a town or fort

lawyer – a person who understands and is trained to practise law

mummified – a dried out body or body part which has not decayed

papyrus – type of paper made from a reed-like water plant

pharaoh – title of the kings of ancient Egypt

portrait – a picture of a person or animal

property – a piece of land that is owned by someone

revenge – punishment made in return for what someone has suffered

stationery – writing materials such as letter-headed paper

transmitting – sending a message between one person or piece of equipment and another

Index

Babylon, King of   6, 7

Bell, Alexander Graham   14

birthday invitation   11

carrier pigeon   22–23

clay tablets   4

Cooper, Martin   25

Dare, Zena   18

des Granges, David   13

Dickin Medal   23

Egyptians   6, 8, 9, 22

email   4, 24, 26–27, 28, 29, 30

First World War   20, 21, 23

Gulf War   22

Hadrian's Wall   10

Hill, Rowland   16

Internet   26, 27, 30

invisible ink   30

King Charles II   12, 13

Mary of Exeter   23

mobile phone   24, 25

National Return Letter Centre   28

Owen, Wilfred   20, 21

Pharaoh Akenhaten   6

postcards   18, 19

postcode   29

Queen Victoria   16, 17

Romans   10

Royal Mail   12, 28

Second World War   23

Severa, Claudia   10, 11

Shepsi   9

stationery   30

telephone   14, 15

texting   24–25

Vindolanda   10, 11